*Essential Training for*

# PREPARING

*for the*

# GLORY

*Essential Training for*

# PREPARING

*for the*

# GLORY

*Getting Ready for the Next Wave
of Holy Spirit Outpouring*

## JOHN & CAROL ARNOTT

DESTINY IMAGE® PUBLISHERS, INC.
P.O. Box 310, Shippensburg, PA 17257-0310
*"Promoting Inspired Lives."*

This book and all other Destiny Image and Destiny Image Fiction books are available at Christian bookstores and distributors worldwide.

Interior design by Terry Clifton

For more information on foreign distributors, call 717-532-3040.
Reach us on the Internet: www.destinyimage.com.

ISBN 13 TP: 978-0-7684-1792-0
Ebook ISBN: 978-0-7684-4305-9

For Worldwide Distribution, Printed in the U.S.A.
1 2 3 4 5 6 7 8 / 22 21 20 19 18

# CONTENTS

# HELLO!

We want to thank you for joining us in our course, *Preparing for the Glory*. In our many years of ministry, we have experienced the Lord's presence in profound and life-changing ways. We believe He wants to bless you with revival in the same way. That's why we created this course: to help you to walk in the power of God as you encounter and steward His glory in new ways.

Over the course of the next eight weeks, you will discover what it means to be anointed of the Lord, how to steward His presence and glory in your own life, and why it's so important to walk in holiness and honor as you pursue the things of God. It is our hope that through this course, He would work in your heart powerfully so you can carry His fire in your heart and into the world!

Thank you again for taking the time to be with us. We are praying each lesson would fan the flame of the Spirit in your life!

Blessings,

John and Carol Arnott

# USING THE STUDY GUIDE

This study guide provides you with eight interactive sessions that you will go through together as a group or class. You may also engage the sessions individually, but you will get the most out of the curriculum content by engaging the sessions in a small group or class experience.

In order to prepare yourself to foster revival in your community, you need reinforcement. The keys that John and Carol provide in both the book and curriculum materials are designed for practical application in your daily life.

In the exercises you will have journaling space follow each of the questions. As you engage each of the exercises, you will move from "glory to glory" in your relationship with the Lord and will be transformed into a growing disciple who learns how to sustain the power of God in your everyday life.

*Session One*

# THE SUDDENLY OF GOD

Did you know the word "suddenly" is mentioned 72 times in scripture? That's because God often works in "suddenlies"—showing up and moving when we least expect it. Jesus Himself came as a suddenly. After the nation of Israel prayed for a Messiah, He *suddenly* came into the world in the most unexpected way: as a baby. This example and so many more reveal the heart of God to come into our lives and bring transformation.

# JOURNAL

# *Week 1*

# VIDEO LISTENING GUIDE

1. _____, _____, and _____
   are examples of God working suddenly in the Bible.

2. A "suddenly" is a turn of _____ that changes your
   _____.

3. Jesus came in power suddenly after He spent 40 days in the
   _____.

4. We can't pay off our debt with _____. Instead, Jesus
   paid our debt with His _____.

5. Romans 8:28 says all things work unto _____ for
   those who _____ God.

# SUMMARY

This week's lesson focuses on how we can prepare our hearts for the suddenly of God. When we are aware of His heart to suddenly bring revival and power, we can be ready and equipped to steward His presence. One day soon, Jesus will come again in power for His bride. Are you ready for this—the greatest suddenly of all?

### *God's Heart to Bring Breakthrough*

Of course, the Lord sometimes works gradually, teaching us about Himself over time. But many times, He comes when we least expect it, bringing about change and transformation. He loves us so much that He ordains times and experiences for us to encounter Him in this way!

To truly prepare our hearts for what's to come, let's look at how God has been faithful in past "suddenlies". Take some time to think about some of the "suddenlies" of your own life. Perhaps you can remember a time when God broke in and brought healing or revealed His heart to you in a new way?

# DISCUSSION QUESTIONS

1.  List a few ways you have seen God "storm in" to your life and change everything.

2. How did God's sudden work in your life shift your paradigm or change your perspective about a situation?

3.  Just as importantly, what have God's "suddenlies" taught you about Him and His character?

4.  What does it say about God that He often shows up when we least expect it?

_____

_____

_____

_____

_____

_____

_____

_____

_____

_____

### *Preparing Our Hearts*

There is a powerful parable in Matthew 25 that speaks to the importance of being prepared for Jesus to come. In the story, there are ten virgins in the story waiting for their bridegroom to come. Of the ten, five are prepared with oil for their lamps, and the other five are not. When the bridegroom comes suddenly in the night, he takes only the five virgins who were wise and prepared. In the same way, we are called to prepare our hearts and lives for the coming of the Lord.

1. In the parable of the ten virgins, who are the virgins, what is the oil, and who is the bridegroom?

2. What are some practical ways we can "prepare" for the coming of Jesus?

_____

_____

_____

_____

_____

_____

_____

_____

3. How would your life be different if you meditated regularly on the second coming of the Lord?

_____

_____

_____

_____

_____

_____

_____

—————————————————————————————————————

—————————————————————————————————————

—————————————————————————————————————

—————————————————————————————————————

## ACTIVATION: LEARN TO RECOGNIZE THE SUDDENLY OF GOD IN YOUR LIFE

Spend time in groups of two or three, and share about a time when God broke in suddenly.

How did this breakthrough compare to times when God worked more gradually or slowly in your life?

What did God teach through His sudden work?

Share with others what God did for you and pray for the same grace to be released with the other members of the group.

*Congratulations—you completed week 1! Let's move on to next week's teaching. We can't wait to explore the Baptism of the Spirit.*

## Session Two
# THE BAPTISM OF FIRE, PART 1

When we join with God in the work He is doing around us, we can grow in power and authority and bring revival to the world around us. As we see in Carol's example of praying over a young girl at church, choosing to partner with God in what He's already doing changes everything. It's His job to bring revival—all we have to do is walk with Him in it!

# JOURNAL

# *Week 2*
# VIDEO LISTENING GUIDE

1. God gave us the Spirit to makes us more like _____ .

2. In the _____ of the Holy Spirit, the Lord imparts His boldness, presence, and _____ .

3. The Lord makes His ministers a _____ of _____ (see Psalm 104:4).

4. God's job in the miraculous is to _____ and our job is to _____ .

5. We are called to _____ the work He starts.

## SUMMARY

In this session, Carol shares about what it means to be baptized in the fire of the Holy Spirit. When He comes upon us, He imparts His presence and power to us so we can live as Jesus lived. The good news is that there's even more of His fire to ignite us! Will we choose to live as a flame of fire for Him?

### *Living as a Flame of Fire*

Psalm 104:4 tells us that God makes His ministers a flame of fire. When we live our lives before Him, postured in worship and ministry to His heart, He ignites us in His power. Let's look at some of the characteristics of fire so we can more deeply understand what this looks like.

## DISCUSSION QUESTIONS

1. Think about the properties of fire. What is fire like? What does it do? How does it work? List out as many properties of fire as you can think of.

_____

_____

_____

_____

_____

_____

2. Now, let's apply these truths to our own lives as we consider what it means to be flames of fire before God. Journal about what it looks like for children of God to take on the properties of fire you listed above. Feel free to get creative in your description!

_____

_____

_____

_____

_____

_____

_____

3.  Think about different manifestations of fire—a small candle, a torch, a fireplace, a fire pit, a forest fire, etc. Which form of fire is your life like right now? Which one do you want to be? How can you get there?

# FANNING THE FLAME OF OUR HEARTS

Oftentimes when a fire starts, it comes powerfully. Then, over time the fire wanes, whether it just dies out gradually or is put out intentionally. As believers pursuing revival, we have responsibility over our own flames. Let's consider how we can become better stewards of our flames.

1. What are some practical ways you can steward your flame? Think about what stirs your affection for God and encourages your heart to worship Him.

_____

_____

_____

_____

_____

_____

_____

_____

2.  On the other hand, there are certain things in our lives that can quench the flames of our hearts. What in your life—attitudes, behaviors, emotions, etc.—tends to put out the flame God has put in your heart?

3.  Now, take some time to write out a prayer asking God to fan the flame of your heart. Ask Him about how you can live a life ignited in the Spirit and if you hear anything, write down what He says.

## ACTIVATION: BEING BAPTIZED IN THE HOLY SPIRIT

If possible, have praise and worship music ready to go—either live or on some kind of audio system.

Share experiences of being baptized in the Holy Spirit. What happened? What changes came in your life as a result?

You might have already experienced a baptism of the Holy Spirit, or you might have not yet had this experience. God always wants to give you a fresh encounter so we pray for a fresh experience with His love and glory.

***Great work! Now let's move on to week 3, where we will learn more about the baptism of the Holy Spirit.***

## Session Three
# THE BAPTISM OF FIRE, PART 2

There are so many reasons to pursue the presence of God. Encounters with God ignite us with His fire and love. When we soak in the Lord's love and come away with a new revelation of who He is, we empower the Holy Spirit to do meaningful work in our lives. From this place we can step out in boldness with His fire on display to the world!

# JOURNAL

# Week 3

## VIDEO LISTENING GUIDE

1. On the day of Pentecost, Jesus sent His _____ _____.

2. Encountering God's _____ helps us grow in boldness.

3. Mark 7:21 says from _____ proceed evil thoughts.

4. The enemy wants to bring us back to a _____ level.

5. Zechariah 2:5 tells us God will be a _____ around us, the _____ in our midst.

## ▌ SUMMARY

It's important to remember that the motivation of our pursuit matters. Many run toward the Lord for His power rather than out of love for Him, which doesn't yield the same results. Only when we direct our hearts toward Jesus in love will we bear the fruit of His power and presence.

### *Growing in Love for the Lord*

Jesus wants us to run toward Him because we love Him, not just because of what we can get from Him. This means we need to focus on His character, not just His actions and gifts.

## ▌ DISCUSSION QUESTIONS

1.  Why does our motivation matter when we seek revival?

_____

_____

_____

_____

_____

_____

_____

2. To stir our hearts in love for God, let's list out some of the gifts He gives us and trace them back to His character and heart.

### Power:

God is _____

### Healing:

God is _____

### Grace:

God is _____

### Signs and wonders:

God is _____

3. List any more you can think of below.

_____

_____

_____

_____

_____

_____

_____

_____

_____

4. Can you think of a time you've approached God in worship and it was fruitful? Describe it here.

_____

_____

_____

_____

_____

_____

_____

_____

_____

_____

## *The Work of The Heart*

Thankfully, we are never stuck in our ways. The Lord's presence is a safe place for us to be transformed in Him. When we unite our hearts to His, He uproots unhealthy motivations and lies we believe so we can walk in wholeness. It's encouraging to remember that even when we come to Him with a wrong motivation, He can make our hearts right. His presence purifies our hearts!

1. In this session, Carol describes soaking in the Spirit as wetting the soil so He can wiggle out bad roots more easily. Can you think of anything in your life the Lord might want to uproot? Take some time to ask Him and write your answer below.

_____

_____

2.  Why does spending time in the presence soften our hard hearts
    and renew our minds?

3. Every season has a different focus. Some seasons are for healing, and other seasons are for running hard after God. Ask God to help you identify which season you are in, and write about it below.

4.  Regardless of what season you are in, how can you carry the glory of God in your heart in a unique way right now?

## ACTIVATION: THANKFULNESS FOR THE GLORY

If possible, have praise and worship music ready to go—either live or on some kind of audio system.

Spend time journaling and reflecting on the bush of fire that Moses encountered.

Reflect on the "bushes of fire" they have seen in their own lives which are obvious signs of God's glory.

How did this glory encounter change their heart and their lives?

After these things are identified and written down, have a time of praise and worship. This is a time to offer up thanksgiving to God, and prepare the way for more.

*God is ready to anoint you with His presence. We can't wait to move forward into next week with you!*

*Session Four*

# HONORING THE ANOINTING

The word "anointing" has an association with oil. In the Old Testament, Samuel anointed Kings Saul and David by putting oil on their heads. Anointing wasn't just a symbol, however. After they were anointed, Saul and David's identities were radically changed. In this way, anointing is an outward expression of a deeper inner transformation that takes place.

# JOURNAL

## *Week 4*

# VIDEO LISTENING GUIDE

1. The Word Messiah or Christ means " _____ _____."

2. John 6:63 says the Spirit gives _____ but the _____ profits nothing.

3. It's important to keep _____ accounts with God.

4. _____ means we can receive anointing from others.

5. The Spirit's power must never be separated from the Father's _____.

## SUMMARY

In the original Greek, the word "Christian" means "little anointed ones." As Christians, we carry God's anointing through the Holy Spirit. His work in us and through us isn't based on our merit. Still, it is crucial we learn to carry our anointing well, respecting it with how we live our daily lives. This is what it means to honor our anointing. Let's explore a little bit more of what it truly looks like to be anointed and some of the practical measures we can take to live as the anointed children we are.

## DISCUSSION QUESTIONS

1.  Just like fire, oil has some unique properties, which John mentioned in the teaching. Write down some of them here.

2.  Now connect the oil used in the Old Testament to the properties of the Holy Spirit, who anoints us in Jesus. [Hint: What do oil and the Spirit have in common, and what does it mean for us?]

3.  The word "Christian," which means "little anointed one" is a diminutive form of "Christ." It also says something about who we are in Jesus. What truths about your identity do you gather from the meaning of the word "Christian"?

4. Why is it so important that we honor our anointing?

_____

_____

_____

_____

_____

_____

_____

_____

_____

_____

### *How to Honor The Anointing*

The most profound way we can honor the anointing we carry is by investing love in everything we do. On the other hand, First Corinthians 13:2 tells us, "If I have the gift of prophecy and know all mysteries and all knowledge; and if I have all faith, so as to remove mountains, but do not have love, I am nothing" (NASB).

1. In many ways, love is both the root and the fruit of anointing—
   the cause of our anointing and the result of it. What does this say
   about God and about us as His children?

   _____

   _____

   _____

   _____

   _____

   _____

   _____

   _____

   _____

   _____

2. How do God's power and love work together in revival?

   _____

   _____

   _____

_____

_____

_____

_____

_____

_____

_____

_____

3. When you think about impartation—passing on the gift of anointing to someone else—what role does love play?

_____

_____

_____

_____

_____

_____

_____

_____

_____

_____

4.  Toward the end of this teaching, John shares four practical ways
    we can check in with our hearts to make sure we are walking in
    love. In your own words, describe what each one of them means
    to you.

    ## Character:

_____

_____

_____

_____

_____

    ## Competency:

_____

_____

_____

**Motive of your heart:**

**Track record:**

## ACTIVATION: HONORING THE ANOINTING

Read Romans 1:11-12. It shows Paul's value for impartation and honoring the anointing.

> *"For I long to see you, that I may impart to you some spiritual gift to strengthen you— that is, that we may be mutually encouraged by each other's faith, both yours and mine"* (Romans 1:11-12 ESV).

Take turns telling one another about the grace and anointing you see in the life of each other.

Pray over each other and impart that grace into one another's lives. Share how it felt to be honored publicly for what you carry.

*Thank you for joining us as we discovered how to honor our anointing! We can't wait to share about the power of honor next week.*

## Session Five

# THE POWER OF HONOR

When Jesus read from Isaiah 61 in the temple, He went public with His anointing. But even as He performed great miracles and taught powerful messages of love, people didn't recognize Him as the Anointed One. In the same way, when we are anointed, others may not see us as God sees us.

# JOURNAL

# *Week 5*

# VIDEO LISTENING GUIDE

1. Pure doctrine is rooted and _____ in love.

2. In Luke 4 Jesus reads from the book of _____ and announces His anointing. But people from His hometown did not see Him as _____.

3. _____ in the Old Testament was truthful about the fact He was anointed by God.

4. There is a difference between _____ and _____ about our anointing.

5. _____ almost missed the blessing of God.

# SUMMARY

It's so important for us as God's children to honor the anointing on others' lives and see people as God does. In the same way, we need not get discouraged or bitter when others don't recognize the anointing on our lives! While bitterness toward others can block the flow of the anointing, honor blesses us, others, and most of all, the Lord.

## *Grace Blockers*

In the beginning of this week's teaching, John shares about "grace blockers," attitudes and behaviors that can block the flow of the anointing God has placed on us. Each one has a specific antidote that can release our anointing. For example, while telling a lie could block the flow of the anointing, honesty would be the antidote.

For each grace blocker listed here, list the corresponding antidote.

Fear: _____

Pride: _____

Obedience: _____

Stinginess: _____

Flesh: _____

Bitterness: _____

# DISCUSSION QUESTIONS

1.  Why do you think "grace blockers" have such a powerful effect on our anointing?

2. How can we get from a grace blocker to the antidote? For example, how do we move from fear to faith? What is the force bridging the two?

_____

_____

_____

_____

_____

_____

_____

_____

_____

_____

_____

### *Honor and the Anointing*

Honor is the antidote to bitterness, a powerful way to protect our own anointing and celebrate others'. However, this doesn't always come easily. We can easily grow bitter when others don't see what God has put on us. With Jesus as our example, though, we can learn to honor and love those who do not see or understand all that God is doing in and through us.

1. How did Jesus respond to those who did not recognize Him as the Messiah?

2. What is the difference between being BOLD with your anointing and BOASTING about your anointing?

3. What does it mean to honor others in their anointing?

4.  It can be easy to disqualify yourself when other people don't honor what you carry. What are some truths you can remind yourself of when you are tempted in this way?

_____

_____

_____

_____

## ACTIVATION: THE ANOINTING IN EACH OTHER

Share areas in life where you are struggling and needing grace in your life.

Have a member who has that grace in their life, pray for strength and grace to be released.

God has placed you in a community of people. Strengthen each other to step into the full promises of God.

*You carry something powerful, and God has designed you to use it for His purposes! We believe God will honor the work you're doing to walk in your anointing.*

*Session Six*

# WALKING IN HOLINESS

God's grace is a wonderful gift to us. But when we focus on His graciousness, it can be easy to lose sight of His holiness. In this teaching, Carol invites us to awaken to the Lord's holiness and allow it to bring us to a place of repentance. When we humble ourselves before Him in obedience and refuse to compromise our character, we will see the signs, wonders, and revivals we have prayed for!

# JOURNAL

# *Week 6*

# VIDEO LISTENING GUIDE

1. God does not want us to take His _____ for granted.

2. The next cloud of glory God brings will be a cloud of _____.

3. The _____ of the Lord is the beginning of wisdom.

4. If we want to see revival, God calls us to walk in _____.

5. Jesus said, "I only _____ what I hear my Father _____. I only _____ what I hear Him _____.

## ▌ SUMMARY

Carol had a dream in which the Lord reveals the powerful effect of small decisions we make in our daily lives. While it may seem like our little compromises don't make a big difference, they actually grieve the heart of God and impact our relationship with Him. They can even keep us from encountering the revival we contend for.

## ▌ DISCUSSION QUESTIONS

1.  The Lord is preparing a bride for Himself. How does your perspective on holiness change when you think about holiness in terms of a bride preparing for a wedding?

2.  Carol mentions that the next move of God will involve His chil-
    dren growing in fear of Him. What does it mean to fear the Lord?

3. Proverbs 9:10 says, "The fear of the Lord is the beginning of wisdom." How are fear of God, wisdom, and holiness related?

_____

_____

_____

_____

_____

_____

_____

_____

_____

4. With the above in mind, how do you think holiness and sin can impact revival?

_____

_____

_____

### *Examining Your Heart*

Now that we understand why holiness is such a valuable currency in the Kingdom of God, let's spend some time examining our hearts before the Lord.

1. Take some time to pray. Ask the Lord to convict your heart of anything in your life that He is wanting to address. Is there an area of compromise He wants you to grow in? Write anything that comes to mind below.

2. Now, as you feel led to do so, repent before the Lord. Confess your area of compromise knowing that He will honor you with forgiveness.

3. Ask God if there is any lie you've believed about Him or yourself that may be contributing to this habit or sin. What truths might He want to speak over you today?

# ACTIVATION: HOLINESS AND GRACE

Individually, take time to reflect on God's holiness and grace. Journal about which of those two you have focused on more in the past and ask God for a fresh perspective on the one you feel less confident in.

Share with the group about where you are needing to grow and develop more insight.

Encourage the people you pray for to actively go after developing this deeper realization throughout the week.

_____

_____

_____

_____

_____

***When you confess your sins to God, you are fully forgiven, washed in the blood of Jesus. Move forward in power and confidence, knowing God sees you as pure and beloved!***

*Session Seven*

# STEWARDING
# THE ANOINTING

S tewarding the anointing means sustaining the fire of God. Rather than a one-time encounter, we can walk in a lifestyle of signs and wonders, boldly stepping into the power of God each day.

# JOURNAL

# *Week 7*

## VIDEO LISTENING GUIDE

1. It's important to have a _____ model in place to sustain the anointing.

2. _____ will go until revival leaders get worn out and carry on.

3. Take God on His _____, not on yours.

4. The book of _____ saw the greatest revival of all time.

5. God wants us to _____ revival, not _____ it.

# SUMMARY

In this interview session, John and Carol share powerful truths and practical insights from their experience on hosting God's presence and fanning the flame of revival wherever you are.

When we take responsibility over the anointing the Lord has brought, He is faithful! Let's work together with Him to sustain what He's started.

### *Creating a Culture of Revival*

Think of stewarding the anointing as creating a revival culture. With the right tools and plans in place, you can co-labor with the Lord to keep the fire burning in your ministry, church, or home.

When you think of the revival you want to see in your environment, what comes to mind? Circle the words that resonate with your spirit the most, or add your own.

| | |
|---|---|
| Signs | Wonders |
| Power | Healing |
| Miracles | Intimacy |
| Love | Growth |
| Worship | Holiness |
| Restoration | Joy |

# DISCUSSION QUESTIONS

1. With these goals in mind, how can you practically plan ahead for keeping the flame of revival ignited?

2. On a deeper level, what are some ways to prepare your heart to sustain revival culture?

_____

_____

_____

_____

_____

_____

_____

_____

_____

3. Why is it so important to work together as a team to steward the anointing?

_____

_____

_____

4. Who at your church, in your ministry, or in your community/
   family could play a role in helping to sustain the revival you've
   contended for?

5. How does asking questions of the Lord support your revival culture?

6. Why is it so important to engage with God in unexpected ways?

_____

_____

_____

_____

_____

_____

_____

_____

_____

_____

7. What does it mean to be a people that say "yes" to God?

_____

_____

_____

_____

_____

_____

_____

_____

_____

_____

## ACTIVATION: HONORING THE ANOINTING

Read Acts 2 at Pentecost and write down what were the roots and the fruits of revival.

What was the root (cause) of this revival? What was the fruit (result) of it?

_____

_____

_____

_____

Pray and ask the Holy Spirit to move in a similar way in your life.

*We have one more week left together! We're so thankful you've invested your time and heart. Let's move on to next week in faith that God will continue to move!*

## *Session Eight*
# RELEASING THE ANOINTING

The Holy Spirit wants to release strategy for the new season. He wants to show us how to partner with Him to pastor and steward the sovereign gift of His presence. Through humbleness and obedience, He will always be faithful to show you the way.

# JOURNAL

*Week 8*

# VIDEO LISTENING GUIDE

1. God wants us to bring the anointing to the seven _____ of culture.

2. Pastoring anointing is different than trying to _____ it.

3. Giving God our _____ time will always bear fruit.

4. Sometimes, all we have to do is open our _____ and be _____ to release the anointing.

5. God wants to see His _____ released in our spheres of influence!

# ▌ SUMMARY

In this final session, John and Carol take time to pray for leaders looking for revival strategy and offer crucial insight on what it means to pastor the anointing. As we keep in step with the Spirit, He will give us the tools we need to sustain a culture of revival wherever we are, and just as importantly, bring it out into the world. Partnered with Him and plugged into the Lord's love, nothing is impossible for us!

As we finish, let's take time to explore what it looks like to carry the anointing He's given us into our spheres of influence.

### *Pastoring the Anointing*

If we want the anointing to thrive and grow, it's important to be intentional and strategic. Rather than following our own whims, God wants us to partner with the work of the Spirit and respond to Him.

# ▌ DISCUSSION QUESTIONS

1. John and Carol use some distinct language here, encouraging us to pastor the anointing instead of controlling it. What is the difference between the two?

2. How can spending time with the Lord regularly help us to strategize and bear fruit in the revival taking place?

3. On a different level, why is it important to pastor our own hearts in the midst of revival and anointing? In other words, how does our own personal revival affect corporate revival?

## *Taking Revival to Culture*

God wants us to step out in faithfulness wherever we are, bringing the revival He has ignited to public spheres. Whether you pray over someone at the grocery store or share the love of God with a family member, the important thing is that you take risks with Him. These small steps of obedience have power to change the world!

1.  How does the revival taking place in your church or ministry impact you and embolden you to take it elsewhere?

2. What area of culture do you feel specifically called to bring His power to? Ask the Lord where He wants you to be influential, and write about it here.

3. God's fire can take many forms. What aspect of God's heart or character do you most want to bring into the space you described above? What would it look like to see revival in this way?

4. As you finish, take time to pray and ask God for one specific takeaway for this season. What truth, strategy, or insight do you feel He wants you to know and carry with you?

---

---

---

---

---

---

## ▎ ACTIVATION: SPHERES OF INFLUENCE

Gather in groups of two or three. Share the areas where you feel like you are supposed to influence and effect.

Spend time praying over each another. Ask the Lord for wisdom on how to release the anointing in your individual sphere of influence and pray over your partner for grace in their sphere of influence.

*Thank you so much for partnering with us for the past eight weeks. We are so thankful you joined us, and we pray God ignites you with His love for a life of passion and power!*

# JOURNAL

# JOURNAL

# JOURNAL

# JOURNAL

# JOURNAL

# LOOKING FOR MORE FROM JOHN AND CAROL ARNOTT?

*Purchase* additional resources—CDs, DVDs, digital downloads, music—from John and Carol Arnott at the online Attwell Bookstore. https://attwellbooks.com

Visit www.johnandcarol.org for more information on John and Carol Arnott, to view their speaking itinerary, or to look into additional teaching resources.

*Become* part of a Supernatural Culture that is transforming the world and *apply* for the **Toronto School of Ministry: http://somtoronto.com/**.

For more information, visit http://catchthefire.com.

# FREE E-BOOKS?
## YES, PLEASE!

Get **FREE** and deeply-discounted **Christian books** for your **e-reader** delivered to your inbox **every week!**

## IT'S SIMPLE!

**VISIT** lovetoreadclub.com

**SUBSCRIBE** by entering your email address

**RECEIVE** free and discounted e-book offers and inspiring articles delivered to your inbox every week!

Unsubscribe at any time.

## SUBSCRIBE NOW!

LOVE TO READ CLUB

visit **LOVETOREADCLUB.COM** ▶